On the mat

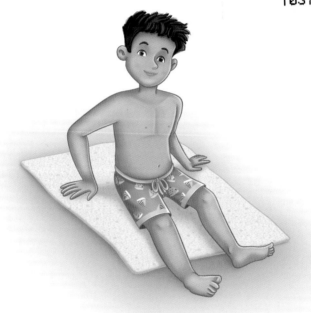

Dan and Sam
ran to the top.

4

Sam got a mat.

Dan did not.

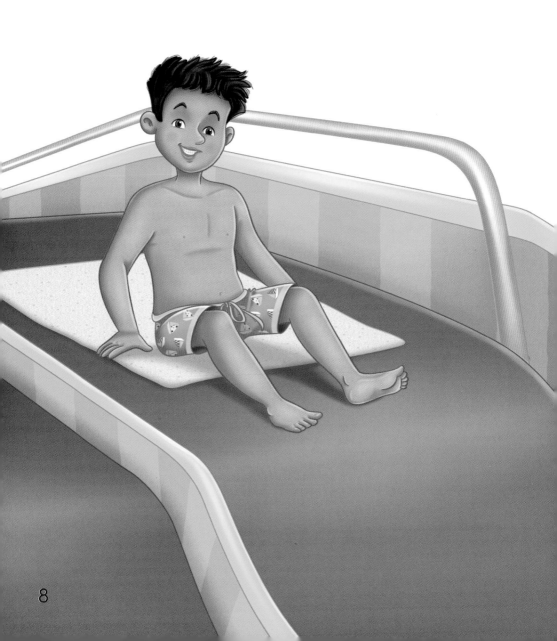

Sam sat on his mat but did not go.

10

Sam let Dan
get on his mat.

Dan got on the mat.

Dan and Sam
had fun.

On the mat

Before reading

Say the sounds: g o b h e r f u l
Ensure the children use the pure sounds for the consonants without the added "uh" sound, e.g. "llll" not "luh".

Practise blending the sounds: mat fun hop sat top ran let Dan Sam

High-frequency words: on and not but got had did get
Tricky words: the no his go to

Vocabulary check: hop – What does it mean to hop? (jump on one foot)
Sometimes when we say "hop in" or "hop on" we mean "get in" or "get on".

Story discussion: The cover shows a waterslide. Have you ever been on a waterslide? What was it like? Did you have to sit on a mat?

Teaching points: Revisit the tricky words "no", "go" and "to". Talk about how the letter o doesn't represent the sound they already know for it, e.g. as in the words "dog" and "top".
Discuss how this story happens in the past so the doing words (verbs), e.g. had, got, sat, have a different spelling.
Note how the "s" sounds like /z/ in the tricky word "his".

After reading

Comprehension:
- Why was Dan sad in the story?
- How did Sam help his brother?
- What would you have done if you were Dan?
- What would you have done if you were Sam?

Fluency: Speed read the words again from the inside front cover.